Hello Badass
Self-Love Coloring Book

You are fucking beautiful, inside and out!

So, get ready to laugh, relax and love the fuck out of your awesome self!

These 30 sweary self-love designs will help you unleash your creativity and embrace your awesomeness! Each design is printed on a single-sided page, so you can use your favorite colored pencils, pens or markers to create fun, unique artwork.

Pro tip: If you're using pens and markers, put another sheet of paper or card stock behind the page that you're coloring to make sure no ink bleeds through. You'll find a test page in the back of the book so you can try out your pencils and pens.

Happy fucking coloring!

Jen@SassyQuotesPress.com

Do you have questions or comments? I would love to hear from you! Please email me at jen@sassyquotespress.com.

 Sign up for freebies and updates at SASSYQUOTESPRESS.COM

Hello Badass Self-Love Coloring Book: Inspirational Swear Word Humor, Sweary Affirmations and Motivational Quotes for Women

Sassy Quotes Press

ISBN: 978-1-957633-66-4

Questions? Comments?

I would love to hear from you! Please email Jen@SassyQuotesPress.com

Ready for your fabulous Bonus Gift?

Go to the **Bonus Gift** page at the back of this book for instant access download info.

Bonus Coloring Pages (printable PDF)

50 Printable coloring pages from some of my most popular swear word coloring books: *Cuss & Color*, *Fuck This Shit*, *You Are Fucking Beautiful*, *Swearing Beauty*, and *The Art of Saying Fuck No*

Sign up for more freebies and updates at SASSYQUOTESPRESS.COM

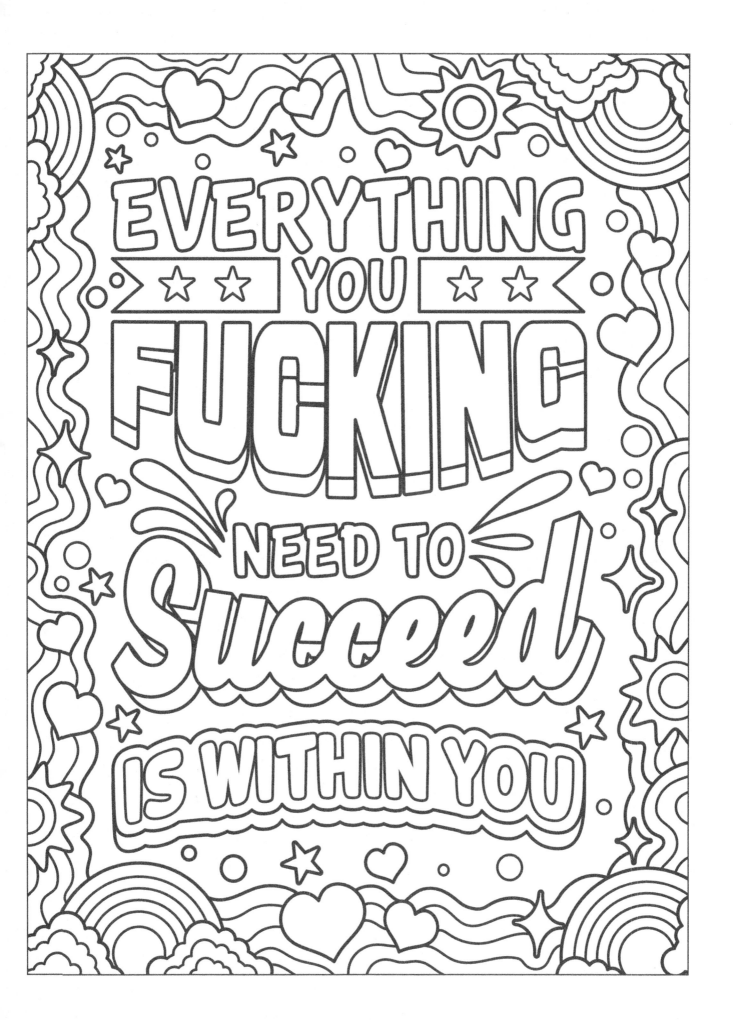

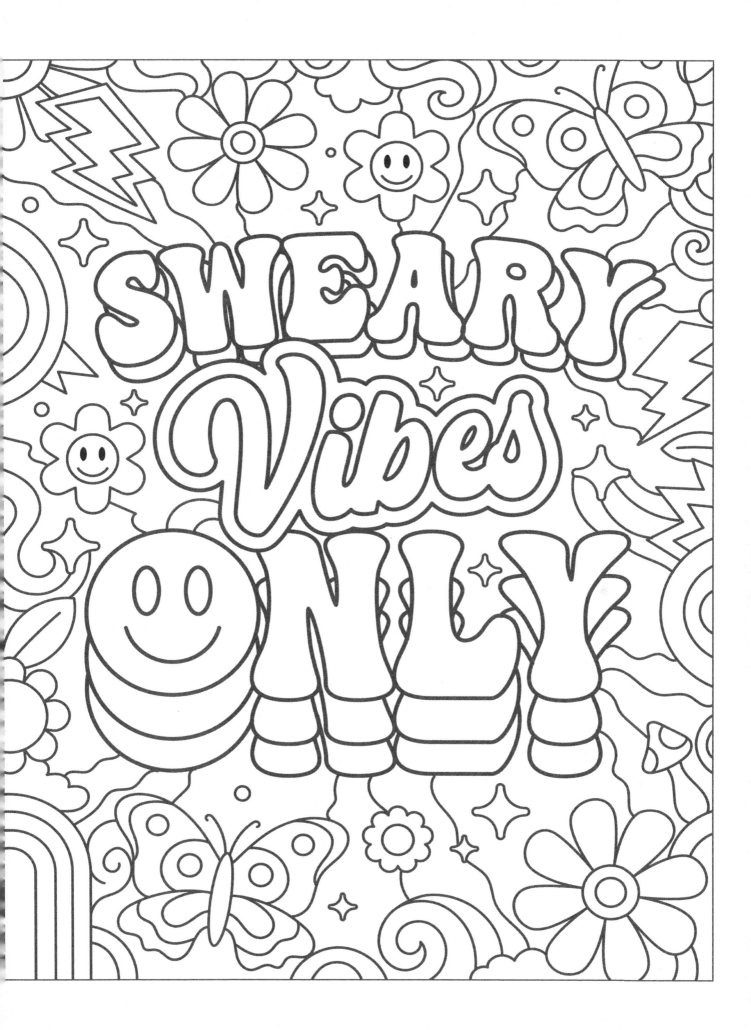

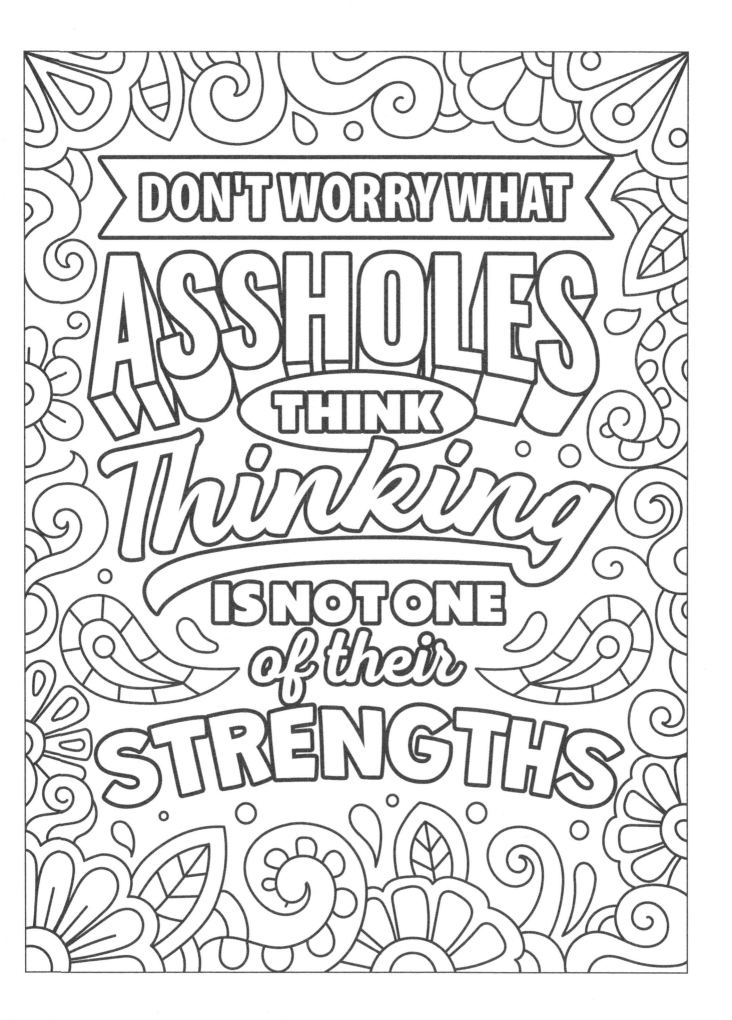

COLOR TEST PAGE

🎁 Bonus Gift 🎁

Hello Awesome! This is a high-quality PDF file that you can print as many times as you like to create a variety of designs. And feel free to share with friends!

What's Included

50 Funny Coloring Pages

Printable PDF (8.5 x 11 in.) with designs from some of my most popular swear word coloring books

How to Access

Option 1

Scan this QR code with your device

You will see a "Download" button for instant access

—OR—

Option 2

Type this URL into your web browser:

sassyquotespress.com/funny1

You will see a "Download" button for instant access

—OR—

Option 3

Email me at
jen@sassyquotespress.com

I would love to hear from you! I can't promise "instant access," but I will respond ASAP!

More from Sassy Quotes Press

Check out more of our hilarious swear word planners, coloring books and gratitude journals. Available on your local Amazon marketplace.

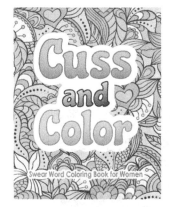
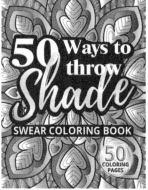

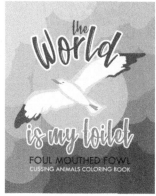
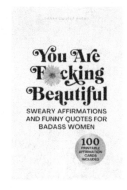

Want freebies and updates?

Sign up for free coloring pages and more at
SASSYQUOTESPRESS.COM

Questions? Comments? I would love to hear from you! Please email me at Jen@SassyQuotesPress.com

☆☆☆☆☆
A Favor Please!

Whether you purchased this book or received it as a gift...

Your star rating or review on Amazon makes a **HUGE** fucking difference to me as an independent publisher.

Seriously. I know your time is *valuable AF*. So, if you could take a quick minute to rate or review my book, I would be *very* grateful!

Two Quick Ways to Rate or Review on Amazon

ENTER IN YOUR WEB BROWSER → https://bit.ly/3AE7UdK

—OR—

SCAN WITH YOUR DEVICE →

Thank you! You are a fucking gem!

Made in the USA
Las Vegas, NV
16 December 2024

14415006R00037